STEAM JOBS IN
FORENSICS

Shirley Duke

Rourke
Educational Media

rourkeeducationalmedia.com

Building Academic Vocabulary and Background Knowledge

Before reading a book, it is important to tap into what your child or students already know about the topic. This will help them develop their vocabulary, increase their reading comprehension, and make connections across the curriculum.

1. *Look at the cover of the book. What will this book be about?*
2. *What do you already know about the topic?*
3. *Let's study the Table of Contents. What will you learn about in the book's chapters?*
4. *What would you like to learn about this topic? Do you think you might learn about it from this book? Why or why not?*
5. *Use a reading journal to write about your knowledge of this topic. Record what you already know about the topic and what you hope to learn about the topic.*
6. *Read the book.*
7. *In your reading journal, record what you learned about the topic and your response to the book.*
8. *After reading the book complete the activities below.*

Content Area Vocabulary

Read the list. What do these words mean?

autopsy
ballistics
elements
entomology
evidence
investigations
liquid chromatography
mass spectrometry
pathologists
residue
rigor mortis
spatter
toxicology
trace

Comprehension and Extension Activity

After reading the book, work on the following questions with your child or students in order to check their level of reading comprehension and content mastery.

1. *Describe the job of a crime scene investigator.* (Summarize)
2. *What can someone's DNA tell about them?* (Infer)
3. *Why might an autopsy be performed?* (Asking questions)
4. *What is rigor mortis?* (Summarize)
5. *How do police retrieve fingerprints from a crime scene?* (Asking questions)

Extension Activity

Does a job in forensics interest you? In the book you read about all the people that are involved in investigating a crime scene. Choose one of those people and do some further research on what qualifications you would need to obtain the job they do. What do you think now? Be sure to record your research in a notebook and go over the pros and cons of a career in forensics!

TABLE OF CONTENTS

WHAT IS FORENSIC SCIENCE?

A man is found dead on the floor of his home. Blood pools around his head. The front door is unlocked. Did he fall and hit his head? Or was it murder?

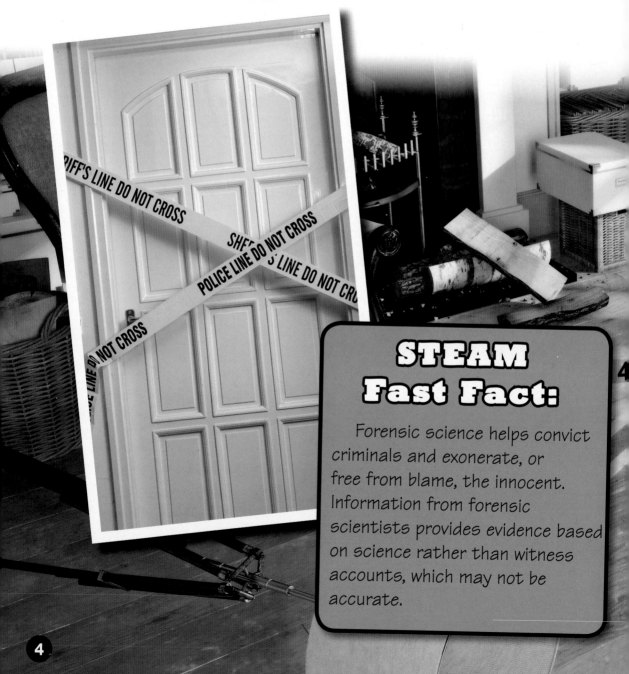

STEAM Fast Fact:

Forensic science helps convict criminals and exonerate, or free from blame, the innocent. Information from forensic scientists provides evidence based on science rather than witness accounts, which may not be accurate.

Forensic science can provide an answer. Forensic science applies scientific methods and processes to solve crimes. Forensic scientists must recognize **evidence**, or a clue, to be able to identify it, and evaluate what it means or where it comes from. This field of study is vital to the criminal justice system.

Forensics covers crimes from murder to bombings to fraud. It provides fair evidence for use in the court system for criminal **investigations** based on objective science.

Crime scene investigators mark evidence using a system of numbers and letters that are positioned, photographed, and recorded.

Science, technology, engineering, art, and math—called STEAM for short—include jobs of all sorts. These fields of study meet people's needs and solve problems. Forensic science incorporates all of the STEAM subjects.

Forensic investigations draw upon the fields of chemistry, biology, physics, geology, psychology, the arts, and the social sciences. Each may play a part in solving crimes. The objective facts come from physical evidence, testing, data, or information collected.

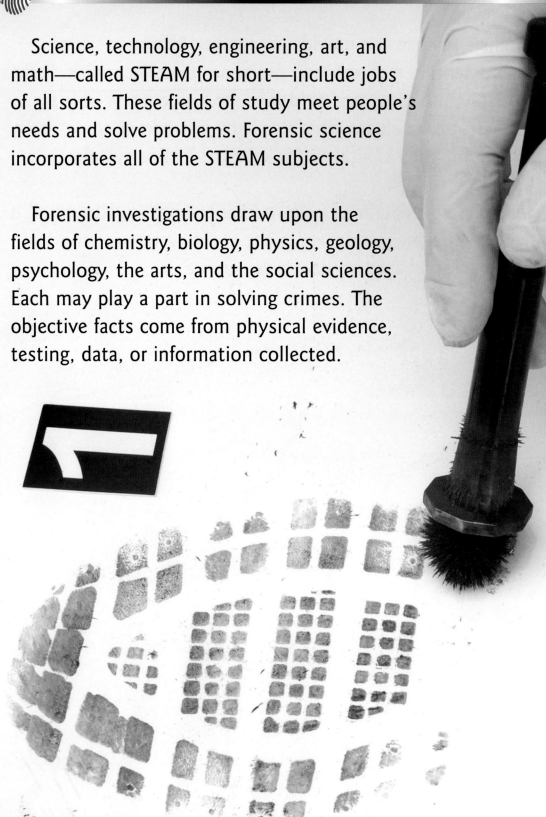

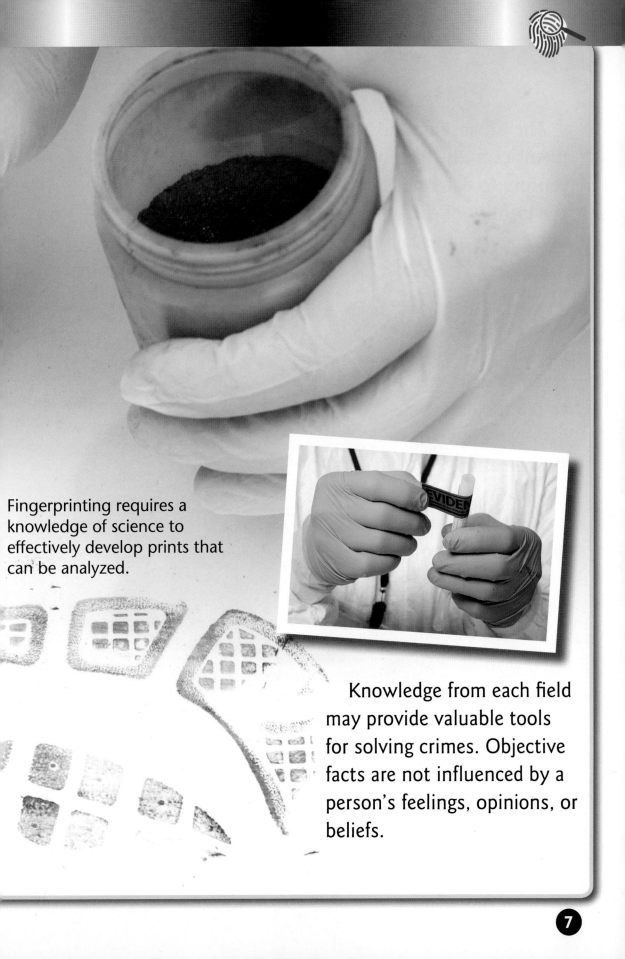

Fingerprinting requires a knowledge of science to effectively develop prints that can be analyzed.

Knowledge from each field may provide valuable tools for solving crimes. Objective facts are not influenced by a person's feelings, opinions, or beliefs.

The Chinese first used forensics in the eighth century to determine the identity of certain documents and sculptures from clay.

In the 13th century, Sung Tz'u's book *Hsi Duan Yu* explained how to tell the difference between drowning and strangulation.

Forensics knowledge advanced rapidly after the 1800s. The late 1900s brought improvements in DNA (deoxyribonucleic acid) testing, which is used to prove a suspect was at a crime scene.

DNA can be collected from hair, blood, saliva, bedding, tools, clothing, and other items.

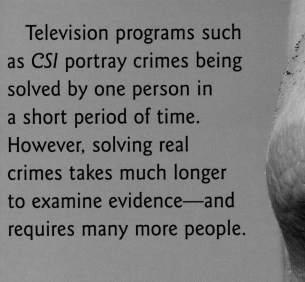

Television programs such as *CSI* portray crimes being solved by one person in a short period of time. However, solving real crimes takes much longer to examine evidence—and requires many more people.

STEAM Fast Fact:

Hsi Duan Yu

Chinese author Sung Tz'u contributed to forensic science by showing how insects can help solve a murder case. The title of his book, *Hsi Duan Yu*, translates to "the washing away of wrongs" and is still read by forensic scientists today.

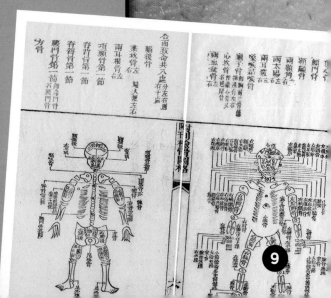

FORENSICS IN ACTION

Art may not be the first thing that comes to mind when you think of criminal investigations, but it's vital to the field. Forensic artists make drawings, reconstructions, or models in clay.

Forensic artists may be certified in composite imaging, facial reconstruction, or age and image enhancement. Composite imaging involves sketching a suspect from a witness's description.

Artists who specialize in facial reconstruction create two- or three-dimensional models of what an unidentified person may have looked like when they were alive.

The Art of Forensic Photography

Forensic photographers use specialized techniques, lighting, and camera angles to accurately capture crime scene evidence. Proper lighting enhances evidence such as blood and fingerprints. They may use high-speed videos for firearm reenactments. Forensic photographers often start as crime scene investigators.

Forensic scientists may specialize in carrying out tests and analyzing evidence. They may work in law enforcement, government, or private forensic laboratories.

Forensic science includes varied jobs. The forensic team consists of many different fields. Forensic **pathologists**, or medical examiners, lead autopsies and collect forensic evidence.

Associated scientists specialize in one area of forensics. They apply the knowledge of their field to analyze and present evidence. The fields range widely, and include **toxicology**, **entomology**, botany, and DNA forensics. Others may focus on tool marks, fingerprints, or firearms.

Trace evidence analysts identify and analyze materials such as hair, fabric fibers, rope, soil, glass, and other materials. Comparing these transferable materials may connect a crime victim to a criminal.

Investigators wear gloves to prevent their DNA from contaminating evidence when collecting it from a crime scene. They are careful to collect, bag, and label every piece of evidence.

Forensic dentists use tooth patterns or bite marks to find out who someone is. This allows victims from crimes, terror attacks, or natural disasters to be identified by their teeth.

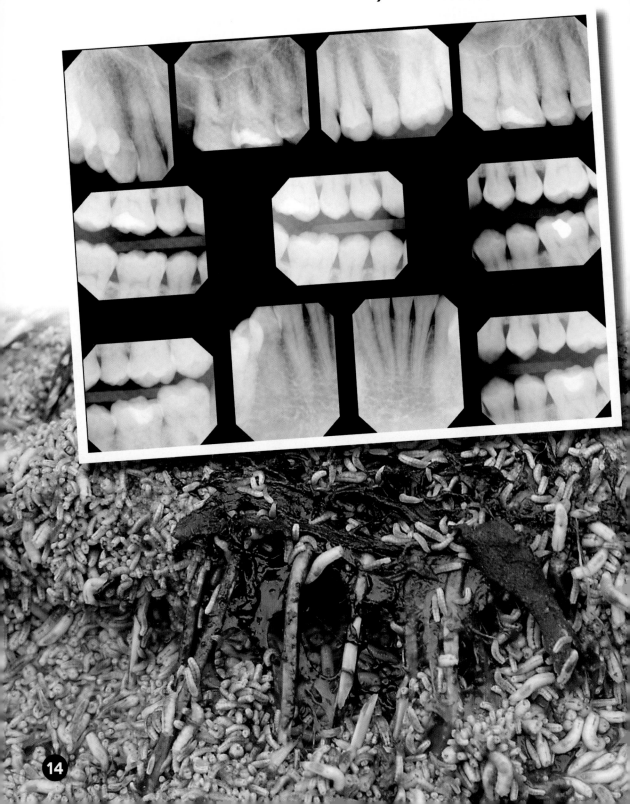

Forensic toxicology includes studying the effects of chemicals or drugs in the body.

Decaying bodies attract insects. By studying the stage of the insect's larval development, forensic scientists can give an idea of the time of death.

Forensic botanists use plant matter to identify where a crime was committed. Plants often come from certain areas or specific ecosystems. This field includes the study of plants, seeds, leaves, wood, fruits, cells, spores, and pollen.

The age of maggots and their stage of development indicate that a body has been dead for less than a month before being discovered.

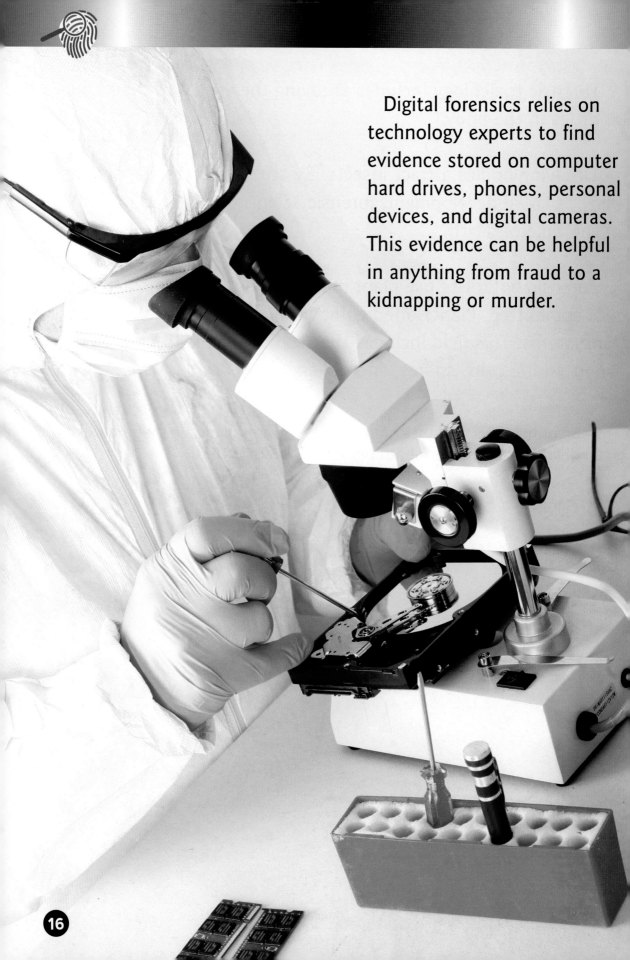

Digital forensics relies on technology experts to find evidence stored on computer hard drives, phones, personal devices, and digital cameras. This evidence can be helpful in anything from fraud to a kidnapping or murder.

Forensic DNA analysis uses DNA samples to identify people. The DNA is removed from the evidence sample, such as blood or saliva. This isolated DNA is processed. It is then compared to a known sample to locate markers that are the same. The use of DNA testing may include identifying a person with a matching pattern or ruling out non-matches.

STEAM Fast Fact:

The Body Farm

The Forensic Anthropology Center in Tennessee, called the body farm, provides research and training for studying human decomposition. Bodies are left outside in the **elements** to observe the process of decay over periods of time.

EVIDENCE ALL AROUND

Biological evidence comes from hair, blood, teeth, bones, and the DNA found in them. Though DNA provides the strongest evidence, hair and its structure add more information. Hair can show race, root evidence, length, and the body part it came from.

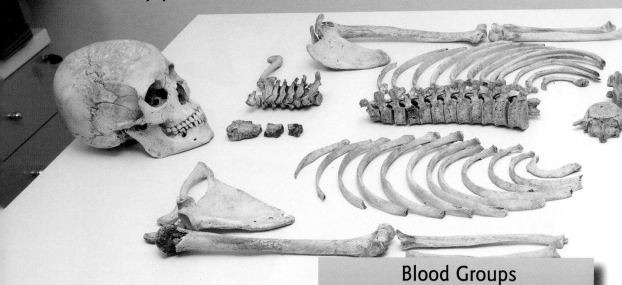

Blood also provides clues. People have a certain blood type—A, B, AB, or O. Blood type can't identify a single person, but it can rule out some.

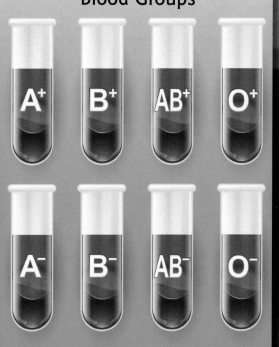

Blood Groups

A⁺ B⁺ AB⁺ O⁺

A⁻ B⁻ AB⁻ O⁻

Forensic scientists use teeth and bones to estimate a person's height, sex, race, and age. The number and condition of the teeth show the age. Bones change as people grow. Older people have more pointed ends on their ribs. The pelvis bones help determine the sex because women have wider pelvises. Skulls may indicate a person's race.

STEAM Fast Fact:

Is it Really Blood?

Sprays such as Luminol and testing sticks called Hemastix are used to identify blood stains. For DNA testing, lab technicians need only a percentage of a drop.

Impressions like **ballistics**, fingerprints, footprints, tire tracks, and blood stain patterns provide evidence. Ballistics experts study holes, wounds, and glass shatters from firearms. Firearms leave rifling marks on bullets. Shells left behind can indicate the type of weapon and details about it. Gunshot **residue**, the faint powder coming from a gunshot, may be found on the shooter's hands or clothing.

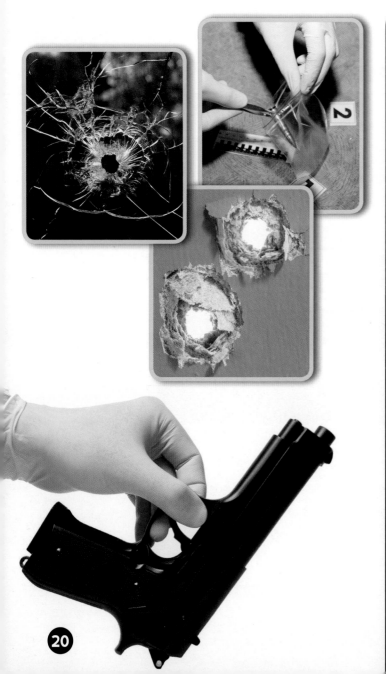

STEAM Fast Fact:

Are You Telling a Lie?

A lie detector test, also called a polygraph, can be used to determine if a suspect is being truthful. The test shows changes in the suspect's heart rate, breathing, and sweating. This evidence is not allowed in court, however.

Blood stain patterns provide evidence from blood **spatter**, or blood being acted on by a force. The patterns indicate the direction the blood traveled and its angle. They show how far the blood traveled and the object that caused the blood to move. Patterns reveal if a struggle took place. The shape of the blood drops indicate how hard the impact was on the victim.

Blood spatter analysis uses biology, physics, and math to analyze and interpret patterns in order to draw conclusions about how the blood got there. Analysts can tell the direction, angle, and sometimes the weapon used from the blood spatter.

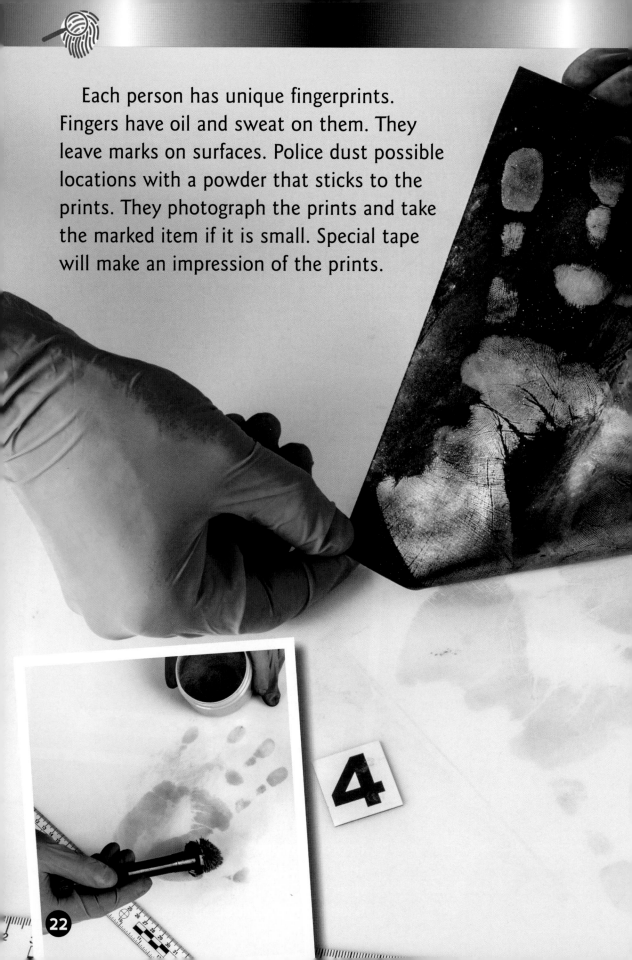

Each person has unique fingerprints. Fingers have oil and sweat on them. They leave marks on surfaces. Police dust possible locations with a powder that sticks to the prints. They photograph the prints and take the marked item if it is small. Special tape will make an impression of the prints.

STEAM in Action!

Dust for Fingerprints

Gather hand lotion, cornstarch or baby powder, a small brush, and cellophane tape. Rub lotion on your hands and press a finger onto a clear drinking glass. Dust the glass with the powder. Using the tape, press it on the fingerprint and lift it. Can you find any other prints you have left in your home?

Crime scene analysts search for items that may have been handled or touched at a crime scene. They dust by brushing powder on the surfaces or use fluorescent dye or powder with a laser or light source in the lab to test for prints. A chemical in super glue is used to protect fragile impressions.

Trace evidence includes fibers, soil, glass, and handwriting studies. Fibers are natural or manmade. Fibers in question are compared to known fibers to compare them. Chemicals treating the fabric are analyzed and compared.

Soil from bodies and shoes gives clues to locations of crimes. Studies look at mineral composition and kinds of matter like pollen found in the soil to hunt for matches.

Shards of glass found in victims or their clothing can be matched on an atomic level and compared with known samples. In forgery and fraud cases, handwriting evidence and impressions left on surfaces under handwritten documents help identify the writer.

PARIS
La Basilique du Sacré-Coeur de Montmartre
Basilica of the Sacré-Coeur of Montmartre
Die Sacré-Coeur Basilika von Montmartre
La Basilica del Sagrado Corazon de Montmartre

Bonjour!
Having a great time! We've seen many sights and walked many miles.

Aïou

4.40

STEAM in Action!

Look at your bathroom sink and shower. Make a list of items you see that would be considered evidence. Do any of them hold material that could be tested for DNA? Name other places in your home where evidence materials might be found.

WHAT HAPPENED?

Often when a person has died, family or friends know who the person is. However, they may not know how the person died. Other times, a body is found and police do not know the person's identity. In both cases, the medical examiner (ME) is called in.

The medical examiner's job is to determine the time the person died and cause of death. To begin, the ME takes the temperature of the body. Upon death, body temperature begins to drop. Temperature falls about one degree Fahrenheit (six tenths of a degree Celsius) each hour for the first 12 hours. After that, the cooling slows to half that time. Clothing, location, and surrounding temperature might make this time vary.

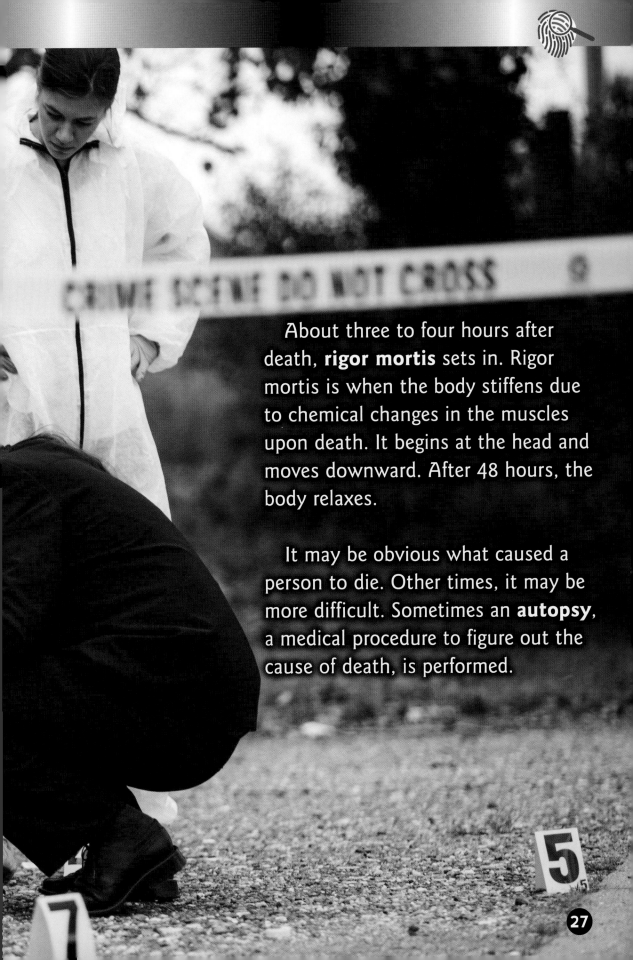

About three to four hours after death, **rigor mortis** sets in. Rigor mortis is when the body stiffens due to chemical changes in the muscles upon death. It begins at the head and moves downward. After 48 hours, the body relaxes.

It may be obvious what caused a person to die. Other times, it may be more difficult. Sometimes an **autopsy**, a medical procedure to figure out the cause of death, is performed.

The autopsy begins with weighing and measuring the body. A photograph and x-rays are taken. Marks that might identify the body, such as scars and tattoos, are recorded. The fingernails are scraped and clipped for evidence, and then the ME takes fingerprints.

Autopsies are performed in a lab called a morgue by medical examiners, who are doctors. The specialized tables allow fluids from the body to drain.

STEAM Fast Fact:
The Science of DNA

Much of DNA is alike in everyone, but parts are unique to each person. Scientists figured out how to identify the parts that differ and compare them to known DNA. DNA is found in sweat, saliva, blood cells, and skin cells.

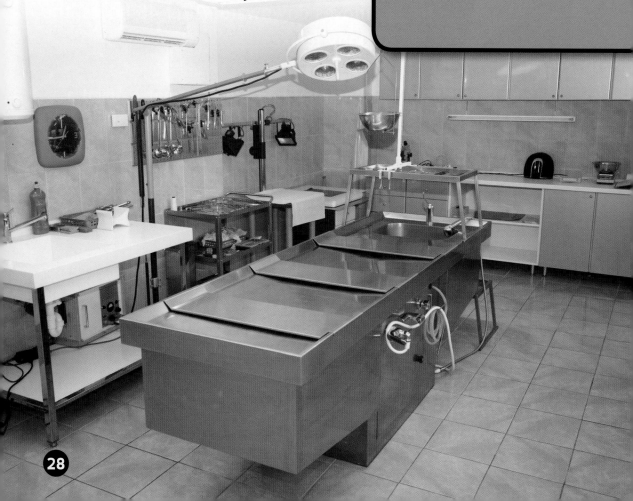

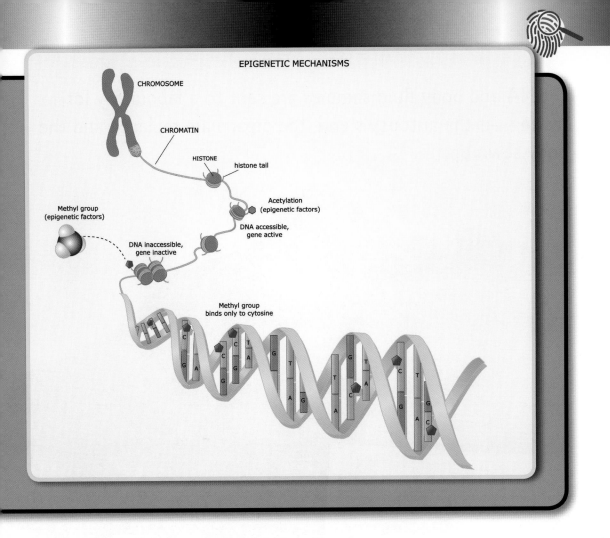

EPIGENETIC MECHANISMS

CHROMOSOME

CHROMATIN

HISTONE

histone tail

Acetylation
(epigenetic factors)

DNA accessible,
gene active

Methyl group
(epigenetic factors)

DNA inaccessible,
gene inactive

Methyl group
binds only to cytosine

MEs also check for fibers or other evidence on the body and collect DNA samples. The body fluids are drained. The organs are removed, weighed, and examined. The head is opened and the brain is removed, weighed, and examined.

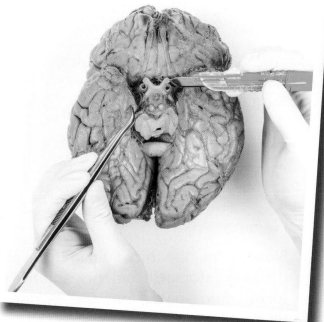

MEs examine the brain to look for traumatic injuries that suggest a blow to the head or for natural causes, such as a blood clot, that might have caused a stroke.

DNA and body fluid samples are sent to a laboratory for testing. At the autopsy's end, the organs are replaced and the body sewn up.

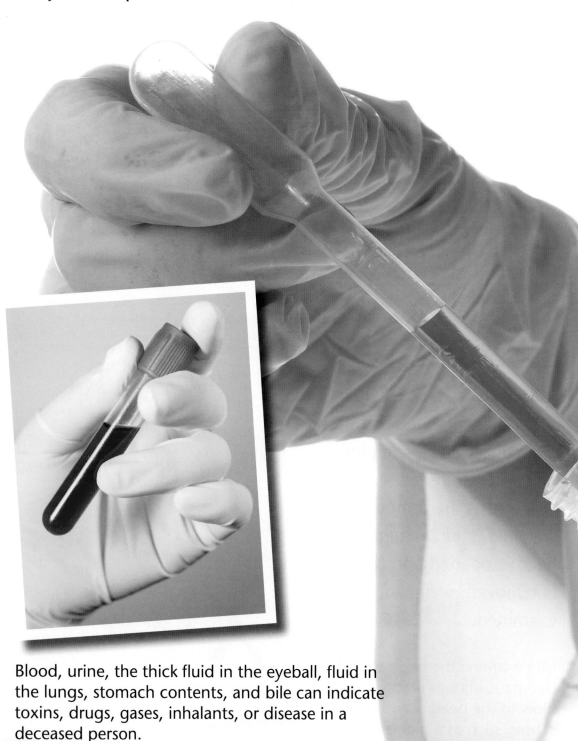

Blood, urine, the thick fluid in the eyeball, fluid in the lungs, stomach contents, and bile can indicate toxins, drugs, gases, inhalants, or disease in a deceased person.

Once the results return, the ME makes a summary of the findings, including the cause of death. The evidence is saved for a trial, if needed. The ME issues the death certificate and the body is released to the family.

SOLVING CRIMES

Police respond to a crime after a 911 call. They use yellow caution tape to secure the location. Securing the area prevents the police or other people from leaving their evidence in that location. Only the evidence present from the crime remains.

A crime scene investigator (CSI) is called in. These investigators are police officers. They work as a team with others. The responding officer communicates with the detective, the CSI, and the forensic specialists.

The investigators are careful not to leave any evidence of their own behind. If they must touch something that will leave their evidence, they make a note of it.

The team interviews witnesses and victims to learn more about the crime. They begin to look for forensic evidence. Bullets, fingerprints, and trace evidence are among the things they look for.

A thorough inspection includes special tools to collect evidence. Police may scrape fingernails for evidence. They vacuum materials from the floor and chairs. Everything is examined.

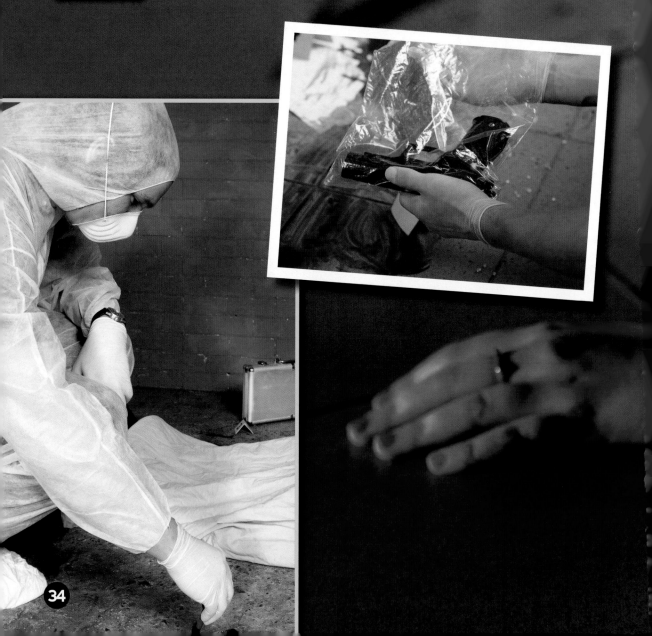

Evidence is photographed and its location noted. Close-up photos are taken to show more detail. Evidence samples are bagged. The bag is labeled and the evidence recorded. Evidence transferred anywhere is recorded on a form. This is the chain of custody. It documents who and when someone had the evidence.

Crime scene investigators use disposable gloves when collecting evidence. They cover themselves with disposable paper suits to prevent leaving their own clothing fibers as they search.

Fingernail scraping collects trace DNA evidence that can be used to identify the criminal or provide other clues in a crime.

Detectives attempt to reconstruct the crime. They look for marks that give clues to what took place. The shape of the marks and their position help police determine what happened and the location of where the criminal was.

Tools used to force open doors or windows leave marks. Bullets leave holes that form a pattern and indicate the order of firing. Blood spatter makes patterns to show angle and direction of impact. Ejected shell cases show the bullet's flight.

Evidence is listed by numbers or letters and labeled, bagged, and documented in a notebook so that it can be studied and presented as evidence in court, if it's needed. Often, the location and order of the evidence provides clues to a crime.

Accurate and fact-based information is important. Forensic scientists work closely with police in the investigations and in court. They provide evidence and give expert testimony. They tell the judge and jury the facts and what they mean. They must defend the evidence they collected.

STEAM Fast Fact:
Crime Scene Reconstruction Engineers

Crime scene engineers use technology, reasoning, and scientific methods to recreate a crime. They can use robotics, 360-degree photographs, and high-tech measuring tools to help them demonstrate the events surrounding the crime. This gives valuable evidence to use in court cases.

TECHNOLOGY OF FORENSICS

Forensic science has advanced from the basic techniques used in the 1800s. Today's forensic scientists have a great deal of advanced technology to use, including 3-D computer imaging.

Liquid chromatography, or the method of analyzing and identifying parts of a mixture, and **mass spectrometry**, the way of identifying the kind and amount of molecules present in a substance, contribute to evidence findings. These techniques analyze evidence down to the level of molecules.

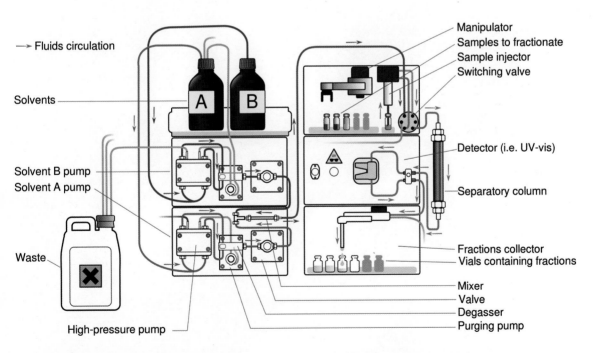

In liquid chromatography, samples are mixed in a solvent and pumped at a high pressure into a column where the components are separated and identified.

Gas chromatography and mass spectrometry let investigators identify very small amounts of toxins in victims or evidence. For example, human sweat is unique to every person. In the future, people may be identified with chromatography using the odor of their sweat.

DNA analysis has made huge improvements in identifying people through saliva, blood, or other evidence from bodies. Scientists using advanced methods of DNA analysis can get results from old or tiny amounts of material as evidence.

Low copy DNA is a sensitive technology to create a DNA profile from a small amount of cells.

STEAM Fast Fact:

Carbon-14 Dating

Body remains can now be tested using Carbon-14 dating. Since all living things contain carbon, special equipment measures the amount of carbon emitted from remains. It has recently become sensitive enough to use on crime victims.

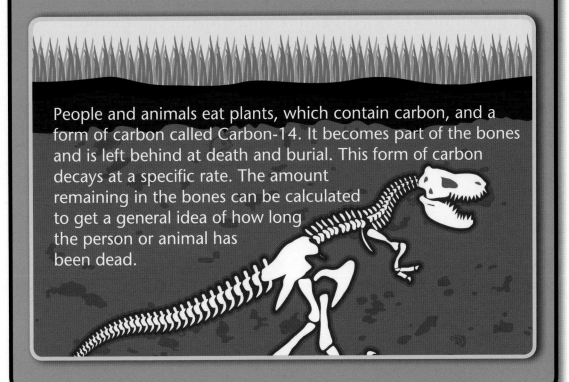

People and animals eat plants, which contain carbon, and a form of carbon called Carbon-14. It becomes part of the bones and is left behind at death and burial. This form of carbon decays at a specific rate. The amount remaining in the bones can be calculated to get a general idea of how long the person or animal has been dead.

R

Forensic radiology uses x-rays, scans, and other technologies to track bullet paths, identify victims, and shape 3-D images of bodies. Live-scan fingerprinting uses a video scanner to change prints to an electronic picture. The scanners quickly compare new prints to fingerprints on file.

Computers are useful for facial reconstruction. A skull is scanned and a facial image is created. This program can also age a person to tell what they might look like as they grow from a child to an adult. This helps police look for missing persons.

Breakthroughs in footprint analysis are being developed. Using the foot's shape and how the person walks may be used in making identifications in the future.

High speed ballistics provides facts about bullet direction, wounds, and glass shatter patterns. Software to detect illegal money transfers help prevent fraud.

Forensic investigations both help identify criminals and exonerate innocent people who were wrongly accused or convicted. The tools and techniques that once seemed the stuff of science fiction are now commonly used in forensic science.

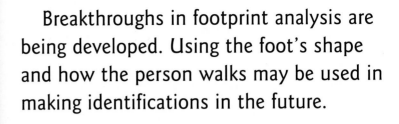

STEAM Fast Fact:

Xbox Forensics

Gaming systems seem harmless, but criminals are known to hide files on Xbox hard drives. Forensic scientists use digital surveillance for Xbox called the SFT Device. This technology lets forensic specialists see the hidden files.

STEAM JOB FACTS

Crime Laboratory Analyst

Important Skills: writing ability, decision making, attention to detail, working well with others, independence, communication, and persistence

Important Knowledge: science, law and government, computers

College Major: chemistry, forensic science, biology, or toxicology

Medical Examiner

Important Skills: critical and analytical thinking, decision making, problem solving, attention to details, flexible, works well with others

Important Knowledge: science, forensics, medical degree, law and government

College Major: forensics, medicine, and forensic pathology

Crime Scene Examiner

Important Skills: precise, organized, good at documenting, evidence collecting, analysis, communication, problem solving

Important Knowledge: fingerprinting, photography, ballistics, science, technology

College Major: forensic science or criminal justice

Forensic Engineer

Important Skills: problem solving, communication, working in teams, confidence

Important Knowledge: engineering, analysis, design, construction, testing, laws

College Major: civil engineering or mechanical engineering

Forensic Artist

Important Skills: drawing, interviewing, accuracy, record keeping, organization

Important Knowledge: composite art, age progression, post mortem and facial reconstruction, computer graphics

College Major: graphics or design

Forensic Photographer

Important Skills: precise, attention to details, record keeping, communication, tactful and discrete

Important Knowledge: photography, digital imaging, image analysis, forensic imaging, choice of proper equipment, police methods, anatomy

College Major: forensic science or forensic photography and imaging

GLOSSARY

autopsy (AW-tahp-see): a medical procedure where a body is examined to determine the cause of death

ballistics (buh-LIS-tiks): the study of how bullets move through the air and the patterns they make

elements (EL-uh-muhnts): the weather, such as wind, rain, and snow

entomology (in-tuh-MAHL-uh-jee): the study of insects

evidence (EV-I-duhns): clues to a crime, such as blood, fibers, and DNA

investigations (in-vest-ti-GAYH-shuhns): gathering information to look into something further

liquid chromatography (LIK-wid krohm-uh-TAH-gruh-fee): a scientific method of analyzing the parts and contents of a mixture

mass spectrometry (MAS spek-TRAHM-uh-tree): the way of identifying the kind and amount of molecules present in a substance using a special instrument

pathologists (path-AWHL-uh-jists): medical doctors that are medical examiners

residue (REZ-i-doo): small amounts of something left over or the remains

rigor mortis (RIG-uhr MOR-tis): the stiffening of a dead body due to chemical changes

spatter (SPAT-ur): splashing or scattering of a fluid after it is acted upon by a force

toxicology (tahk-si-KAHL-uh-jee): the study of poisons and how they act

trace (trays): a very small amount of something left behind

INDEX

SHOW WHAT YOU KNOW

1. Explain why there are so many different divisions of forensic science.
2. What set of responsibilities do forensic scientists have and why?
3. Discuss who works at a crime scene and explain the value of working as a team.
4. Why is evidence and preventing contamination so important?
5. What is the value of using forensic science?

WEBSITES TO VISIT

www.pbskids.org/dragonflytv/show/forensics.html

www.sciencekids.co.nz/sciencefacts/forensicscience.html

www.idahoptv.org/sciencetrek/topics/csi/facts.cfm

ABOUT THE AUTHOR

Shirley Duke is the author of many different kinds of science books. The science of forensics relates to her interest in human biology. Though she won't likely become a crime scene investigator, she enjoys studying the ways science helps solve crimes.

Meet The Author!
www.meetREMauthors.com

PHOTO CREDITS: Cover images: cogs © Keepsmiling4u , fingerprint and dials © deepadesigns, crime scene graphic © rudall30, evidence © Couperfield, photogrpaher © anthonysp; fingerprint icon page header © IhorZigor; page 4-5 © Digital Storm, page 4 © Peter Gudella; page 6-7 © kilukilu, Couperfield; page 8 mouth swab © Henrik Dolle, blood in test tube © science photo; page 10-11 step-by-step reconstruction © Cicero Moraes, 2D reconstruction © Karen T. Taylor (KTT), actual model © Damavand333, photography shot p11 © SensorSpot; pages 12-13 green shirt © Leah-Anne Thompson, tweezers © Petretei, glass with brush © franz12, glass in bag © franz12; page 14 © Steve Wood, page 15 © TimVickers; page 16 © mikeledray, page 17 © Couperfield; page 18-19 © Picsfive; page 20 bullet hole glass © frees, painted wood © Steve Collender, bullet © franz12, gun © Serdar Tibet, polygraph © Andrey Burmakin; page 21 blood smear © Photographee. eu,bood spatter © Couperfield; page 22-23 © afro; page 24 footprint © Sahapon Pongpiansakun, muddy shoes © Polarpx, page 25 © Janaka Dharmasena, Hanka Steidle; page 26-27 © LukaTDB; page 28 © © Picsfive, page 29 © Ferenczi Gyorgy, dan diagram © ellepigrafica; page 30 © EsHanPhot, nimon; page 31 © nimon; page 32 © Prath, page 33 © Photographee.eu; page 34 © Corepics VOF, Photographee.eu, page 35 © Prath, Photographee.eu, Corepics VOF; p36-37 numbers ©bibiphoto, bullet casing © afro, window © sdecoret, blood © Photographee.eu; page 38 © Photographee.eu, jury © bikeriderlondon, page 39 © YassineMrabet, Hannes Röst and M. Steiner.; page 40 © nesBazdar, page 41 © Top Vector Studio; page 42 © sfam_photo, All images from Shutterstock.com except photographer on cover, book pages on page 9, all images pages 10-11, maggots pages 14-15, all images pages 28-29, page 39

Edited by: Keli Sipperley

Cover and Interior design by: Nicola Stratford   www.nicolastratford.com

Library of Congress PCN Data

STEAM Jobs in Forensics / Shirley Duke
STEAM Jobs You'll Love
  ISBN 978-1-68191-742-9 (hard cover)
  ISBN 978-1-68191-843-3 (soft cover)
  ISBN 978-1-68191-935-5 (e-Book)
Library of Congress Control Number: 2016932705

Printed in the United States of America, North Mankato, Minnesota

Also Available as:

ROURKE'S
e-Books